RIOT!

or

This Bloody Crew

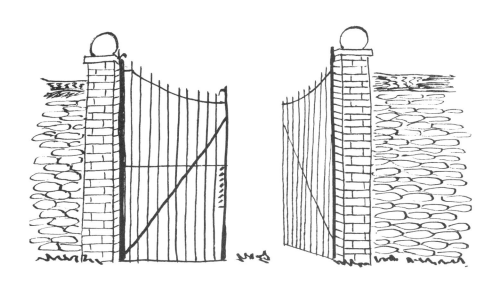

a historical play

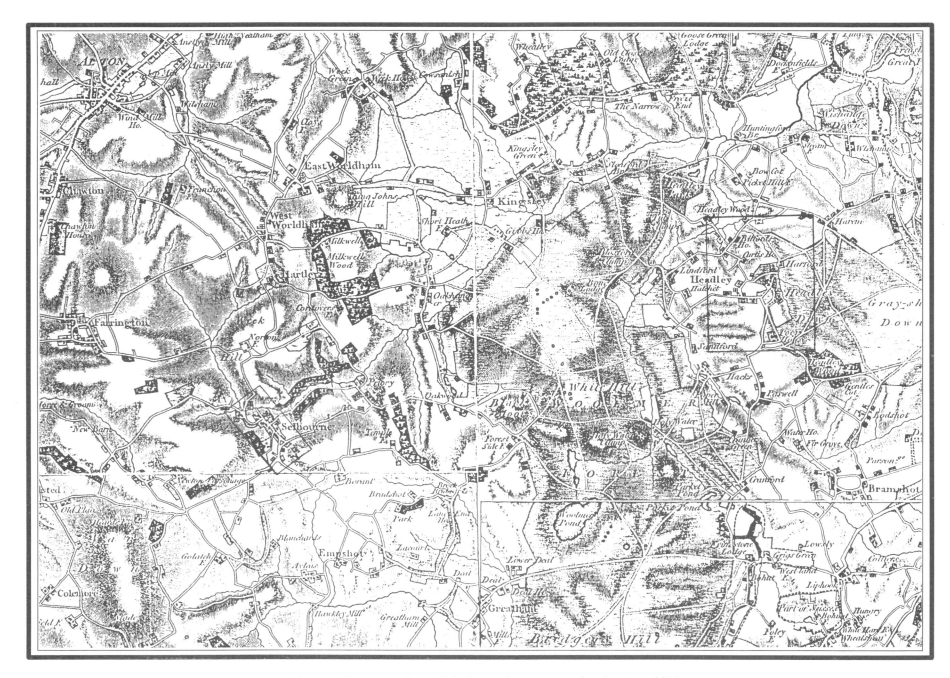

Alton - Liphook area: from 1" Ordnance Survey maps dated prior to 1815

Author's Note

In 1992 I was asked by East Hampshire District Council to write a community play on the subject of the Selborne workhouse riot of 1830. Since I live in the neighbouring village of Headley, I was well aware that we'd also had a workhouse riot in the same year, and rumour said the people who did it came from Selborne. "Typical!", I thought. I knew very little more than that, but it seemed to me that it would be interesting, and still within the terms of East Hampshire's brief, to trace the connection between the two events in the play.

The result was first performed in October 1993 at Selborne, Bordon and Headley, using local actors and musicians.

While the dramatisation attempts to present the known facts as faithfully as possible, any play must inevitably compromise in at least two ways - firstly it cannot accommodate a 'cast of hundreds', and secondly it has to put invented dialogue into the mouths of historical characters.

As an example of the first, I have used only one Selborne farmer in the play - Charles Fitt representing the dozen or more who were actually there on the day - and other similar devices limited the cast to manageable proportions. But the 'Headley 7' are all present, and so is the unfortunate Vicar of Selborne at the time, William Rust Cobbold, around whom so much of the story revolves.

For those who may wish to use this play as historical source material, I have compiled a short appendix which relates the characters and actions of the drama to the true facts as we know them. I have also published a separate book, titled **One Monday in November***, which gives background and references to the material I used when writing the play.*

John Owen Smith
Headley, 1993

One Monday in November ...

... in the year 1830, a mob several hundred strong attacked the workhouse in Selborne, Hampshire, turned out the occupants, burned or broke the fittings and furniture, and pulled down the roof. The next day an even larger mob, containing some of the Selborne rioters, did the same to the workhouse at Headley, some 7 miles away. The parsons in both villages were also coerced into promising to reduce by half the income they took from tithes.

Less than a month later, at a special court hearing in Winchester attended by no less a person than the Duke of Wellington, nine local men were sentenced to transportation (commuted from a death sentence in the case of eight of them), and all but one sailed for the antipodes in the Spring of 1831 never to return.

These are the bare bones of the story. But why did the riot start? Why were the two workhouses attacked? And why were some of the supporters and leaders of the mobs seen to be not oppressed labourers, but relatively well-to-do artisans and farmers?

In this story we cover the dramatic events of the two days and their aftermath, following our band of local men as they march along the lanes and tracks of East Hampshire, to do what they can to relieve their poverty ....

Acknowledgements

The play was first performed in October 1993 under the title *'This Bloody Crew'*, directed by Paul Roberts of the Selborne Players. This followed many months of hard work by both him and John Guest in taking my original text and making it workable. It is not for nothing that John lives in a house called 'Trimmings'! The hardy remains, which you see here, should rightly bear their names as co-authors; and I will be the first to admit that the outcome is a great improvement on the script which I initially offered them.

I have acknowledged within a previous publication, **One Monday in November**, the many people and sources from whom I gathered the information to write this story. I would like to repeat my thanks to them, and particularly to Julia Fry, of East Hampshire District Council, who first put to me the idea of doing this project, and supported it so positively throughout.

My thanks also to the original cast, local people from Selborne, Headley, and surrounding areas, who gave up so many of their Sunday evenings during the summer of 1993 to make it all come to life on the stage; and to Dil Williamson who managed to keep track of the evolving script for us as we headed unremittingly towards the production date.

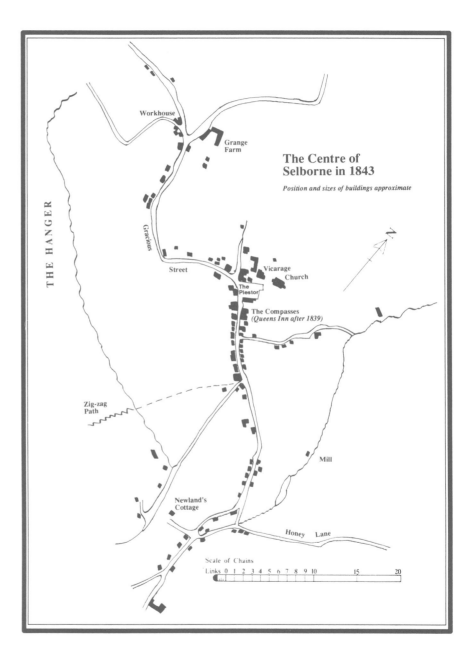

THE HANGER

Workhouse

Grange Farm

The Centre of Selborne in 1843

Position and sizes of buildings approximate

N

Gracious

Street

Vicarage

Church

The Plestor

The Compasses
(Queens Inn after 1839)

Zig-zag Path

Mill

Newland's Cottage

Honey Lane

Scale of Chains
Links 0 1 2 3 4 5 6 7 8 9 10   15   20

- THE CAST -

William Cobbett, radical author and politician

_____

John Cobb, 27, Selborne labourer

Aaron Harding, 41, Selborne labourer

Thomas Harding, 32, Kingsley labourer (Aaron's brother)

John Heath, 45, Carpenter of Selborne (born in Headley)

Robert Holdaway, 37, Carpenter, wheelwright, hop-planter, publican of Selborne

Sarah Holdaway, 27, his wife

Henry James, 38, Brazier, tinman, knife-grinder, soldier

John Newland, 39, Selborne labourer (the 'Trumpeter')

Ann Newland, 32, his wife

James Painter, 36, Kingsley labourer

Matthew Triggs, 37, Bricklayer of Headley

William Triggs, Matthew's brother

_____

Rev William Rust Cobbold, 54, Vicar of Selborne

Mrs Maria Cobbold, 54, his wife

Housekeeper of the vicar at Selborne

Charles Fitt, 72, Selborne farmer

Timothy Loe, 41, Clerk to Selborne vestry

John Harrison, Master of Selborne Poor House

Mrs Harrison, his wife

Harry Harrison, their son

Rev Robert Dickinson, 61, Rector of Headley

Mrs Dickinson, his wife

John Lickfold, 25, Shopkeeper of Headley

James Shoesmith, Master of Headley Poor House

Mrs Shoesmith, his wife

Eli Smith, Headley farmer

Mr Sparrow, a Visitor of the Poor at Headley

Mr Tend, foreman of decorators at Headley Rectory

Richard Rook, labourer of Headley

_____

Mrs Budd, wife of the magistrate Henry Budd

Captain of 5th Dragoons, at _The Anchor_, Liphook

Mrs Dowling, Landlady of _The Anchor_, Liphook

Baron (Sir John) Vaughan, Chief Judge of Special Commission

Sir Thomas Denman, Attorney General at the trials

Usher, at the trials

Gaoler on the prison hulk _York_ at Gosport

_____

Narrators, Mob members, Bystanders, Soldiers, etc.

Singers, Musicians, as required

Several parts may be doubled - see Production Notes.

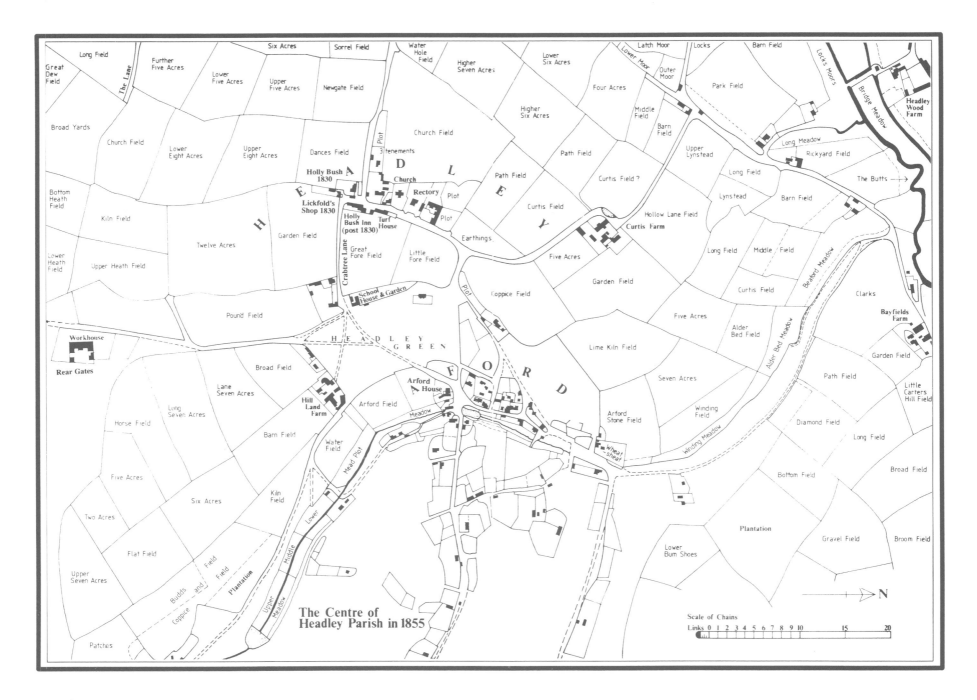

The Centre of
Headley Parish in 1855

Scale of Chains

Links 0 1 2 3 4 5 6 7 8 9 10   15   20

iv

1. On the Hulk 'York' at Gosport

Five of the 'Headley Seven' sit on benches in a gloomy prison cell. Outside we hear sounds of a harbour. Suddenly the Gaoler enters with Thomas Harding and James Painter, in chains.

Gaoler In you go.

Aaron Harding Thomas! James!

Heath *(Ironically)* Thought you were never coming.

Gaoler I'll leave you all to get acquainted again. *(Exits)*

Henry James We're better off than those two they made us watch swing at Winchester.

Holdaway One was only a lad too. All he'd done was knock the hat off a magistrate.

Thomas Harding He must have done more than that.

Holdaway Not by all accounts.

Matt Triggs They should be locked up, not us.

Heath Bastards!

Painter No way we could ever win, was there.

Thomas Harding *(Ironically)* <u>Aaron</u> thought there was.

Aaron Harding *(Turning on him)* What would you do, brother? Just stand there and take charity all your life?

Holdaway *(Angry)* At least your children had you to look after them before - now they're left with nobody.

Aaron Harding There's talk from a vestry member! They'll learn to survive. That's all you do when you're a labouring family - just survive.

Holdaway I'm not a vestry member any longer, Aaron. We're all in the same boat.

Painter And all because of a bloody row.

----

2. William Cobbett rides through Selborne, 7th August 1823

We see William Cobbett in a spotlight, quoting from his Rural Rides.

Cobbett "Seventh of August, 1823. After Tisted, I entered a lane which, at the end of about four miles, brought me to the village of Selborne. I came generally uphill till I got within half a mile of this village, when, all of a sudden, I came to the edge of a hill and looked down over all the larger vale of which the little vale of this village makes a part."

He sees a local Selborne man leaning on his gatepost, and stops to talk to him.

Cobbett Tell me, am I on the road for Selborne?

Man You are. Right ahead of you, down there.

Cobbett Thank you. You must consider yourself very fortunate, living in such a beautiful locality as this. God seems to have done everything for you here.

Man Fortunate? There's not a more unhappy place in England than this village.

Cobbett Unhappy? How so?

Man Oh, there's always quarrels of some sort or other going on in Selborne.

Cobbett On what matters?

Man Matters of rates and tithes mostly.

Cobbett Now I recall, I heard of shots being fired at your vicar, did I not?

Man Aye, but no-one was ever caught.

Cobbett Hardly the story of a parson at ease with his flock.

Man Old Cobbold? Not he - there's not a person here with a good word for him.

Cobbett moves on towards Selborne.

----

3. A meeting of Vestry members in Selborne, November 1830

Holdaway, Fitt and Loe are in heated discussion, seated round a table in a back room of 'The Compasses' in Selborne.

Loe That man Cobbold will have to go!

Fitt Easier said than done, Timothy.

Holdaway Only Magdalen College can get rid of a vicar here.

Fitt Or a bullet.

Loe He's as stubborn as a mule, and arrogant to boot.

Holdaway He certainly keeps his distance from the rest of us.

Fitt And we from him - we know he'll not come to vestry meetings if we hold them in *The Compasses*.

Holdaway It's no distance from the vicarage.

Fitt But it hardly helps when we wish to discuss tithes and rates with him.

Loe He'll have to discuss them sooner or later. The village is about to explode.

Holdaway The village has been about to explode for years.

Fitt Two disastrous harvests, rising prices and no relief on the taxes.

Loe Too much going to the church ...

Fitt From which we get very little back in return.

Loe Not in Selborne anyway.

Holdaway I've heard this before - last year, the year before that ... what makes 1830 so different?

Fitt Hops down to 200 cwt an acre, that's what's different. We expect over a thousand in an average year. You of all people should know how this village depends on hops, landlord.

Loe And unrest in the air. Cobbett's *Register* predicted trouble this winter.

Holdaway 'Better be a dog than a farmer this winter', he said.

Fitt As a farmer, I'm not sure I find that very helpful.

Holdaway We're on the same side here, Charles. We all have to pay rates on our property.

Fitt I'll be meeting the other farmers to suggest we make a proposal to the vicar.

Holdaway Being?

Fitt To negotiate. If he reduces his demand for tithes from the farmers, then we'll pledge an increase in wages to our labourers.

Loe And then we all pay less into the Poor Rate.

Fitt That's a possibility.

Holdaway Only a possibility?

Fitt It's not for me to say. That's for Vestry to decide.

Loe We are Vestry.

Holdaway Us and several others, Timothy.

Fitt We three hardly hold a majority vote.

Loe Who else is going to disagree?

Fitt Who knows? Harrison administers the Poor House; he's hardly likely to relish a reduction in his income.

Loe He's another one who should be looking out for himself.

Fitt You could be right. *(Rising)* And now if you gentlemen will excuse me, I shall go and visit my fellow farmers. I'll let you know the outcome straight away. *(He exits)*

Loe I'll tell you the outcome now.

Holdaway Your a pessimist, Timothy Loe.

Loe With a vicar like Cobbold in the village, there's little room to be anything else.

———————

Erratum: p.2 - As every good hop grower will know, the range of weights should be 2 to 10 cwt. per acre, not 200 to 1,000 cwt. as stated.

RIOT! © 1993 *John Owen Smith*

4. In Selborne Vicarage, morning of Saturday 20 November

We see the Vicar engrossed in writing his sermon for Sunday. The theme is 'Tolerance'. He is reading out loud to himself what he has written so far.

Vicar ... and so I say to you brethren, "Pause" *(he holds up both hands at this)*, pause in what you are doing and consider the dire consequences of your folly. Consider the lilies of the field ...

We hear a door slamming off-stage, and his wife suddenly bursts in.

Mrs Cobbold Mr Cobbold, I am sorry to burst in on you like this without warning, but I must speak with you urgently.

Vicar You are aware that this is the time - one might almost say the sacred time - which I set aside each week, in order to prepare my sermon for the Sabbath.

Mrs Cobbold Indeed, and it is only the most extreme circumstances which force me to break in upon your coveted solitude. I have received warning.

Vicar *(Light sarcasm)* What manner of warning is this?

Mrs Cobbold That we are to be attacked, in this very house, and within the next few days.

Vicar Idle village gossip!

Mrs Cobbold No sir! From a most reputable source.

Vicar This being?

Mrs Cobbold From Mrs Newland. She made a point of taking me aside - saying she would not like to see me or my children come to harm.

Vicar But as for the vicar himself, she has no such concern.

Mrs Cobbold I am sure she did not mean ...

Vicar Are we now to take instruction from the wife of a farm labourer?

Mrs Cobbold She had only our best interests at heart.

Vicar The labouring class have only one interest, Mrs Cobbold, and that is to procreate beyond all reasonable measure and then expect respectable members of society to maintain the offspring of their lustful activities. Since I am the only Gentleman in Selborne, I think ...

Mrs Cobbold There was one thing more.

Vicar Then quickly woman - this sermon will not write itself.

Mrs Cobbold She said we were due for a visit from Captain Swing.

Vicar It is not a name familiar to me.

Mrs Cobbold Nor me - but Mrs Newland seemed to have heard it before. It was the way she looked at me as she said it.

Vicar Madam, this is a most tiresome interruption.

Mrs Cobbold Yes, that is so - but ...

Vicar But in order to placate you, I shall send James with a letter to Mr Budd the magistrate at Liphook, and acquaint him with this tale.

Mrs Cobbold I think that would be well. *(She exits demurely)*

Vicar *(To himself)* How has this living become such purgatory? I feel my very life is threatened each day I remain here. I shall buy myself a mastiff for protection - a mastiff with a neck as thick as a lion's. *(He sighs and resumes work on his sermon)* "Consider the lilies of the field." I think not. *(He crosses it out, and continues writing as the scene ends)* "Consider the Gadarene Swine ..."

---

5. At Selborne Workhouse, afternoon Saturday 20 November

The farm labourers are receiving that part of their weekly wage given out of the Poor Book - they each have a Ticket from their employer which they present to Mr Harrison. We see Aaron Harding receiving his dole.

Harrison Right, who's next? Come on - line up, line up! *(He hands Aaron Harding his dole)*

Aaron Harding Is that supposed to keep me and six children alive for a week?

Harrison Grumbling again, Harding - all you ever do, grumble.

Aaron Harding And with good cause. It's hardly worth standing in line for that.

Harrison Would you like me to give it to the next man then? I'm sure he'd be more than grateful to take it.

Aaron Harding It's hardly enough to buy a daily loaf of bread these days. How can seven of us live on one loaf of bread a day?

Harrison None of my business - I just give out the dole - I don't fix what it should be. Now move on.

Aaron Harding Some of us are going to go round to the farmers and make them raise their wages.

Harrison I'd strongly advise you not to do so.

Aaron Harding Hoo! You don't have to live on nine and six a week - alright for you to *(mimics him)* strongly advise us not to do so.

Harrison You'll regret it if you do - you and the rest.

Aaron Harding You're not best loved in this village Mister Harrison, you know that don't you.

Harrison Get out and let the rest in.

Aaron Harding I'm going - but you watch out. It may not be just the farmers we visit! *(He goes away)*

Harrison Right, who's next?

General light fades and Narrators stand downstage in spotlights.

Narrator 1 In November 1830, the scale of minimum wages paid in Alton was based on the price of a gallon loaf of bread, which at that time cost one and sixpence halfpenny. An Alton labourer's family was entitled each week to a gallon loaf per head and one over

Narrator 2 So a widower like Aaron Harding with six children below working age in Alton would be entitled to the equivalent of eight loaves a week, or twelve shillings and fourpence in parish dole. If he was unemployed, he would receive all of this from the parish dole.

Narrator 1 If he worked, he could earn around 8 or 9 shillings a week from his employer, and then only the balance would be paid from the parish dole. In other words, whether he worked or not, he would receive his twelve shillings and fourpence a week, no more and no less. A poverty trap from which he could not escape.

Narrator 2 Minimum wages in Selborne appeared to be even less than those in Alton. Records show Aaron Harding, 3 years earlier, receiving just twelve shillings a week from the dole for himself, his wife and six children. When his wife died, this would have been reduced by 2/6d to just 9/6d a week - the equivalent of about six gallon loaves of bread.

---

6. A Room in *'The Compasses'*, evening Saturday 20 Nov.

Robert Holdaway, Aaron Harding John Heath and John Newland are sitting round a table. Holdaway has a copy of William Cobbett's 'Political Register' with him.

Holdaway I don't like it any more than you do John, but there's news of risings succeeding in other parishes, and we can't ignore it.

Newland Why do we have to react to what happens in other parishes? We're grown men - we can make our own decisions. Taking action now can only bring pain and misery.

Aaron Harding There's already pain and misery. Folks can't sink any further - they've got nothing to lose now.

Heath We should use our strength - all rise together and teach the gentry a lesson they won't forget.

Holdaway You're talking with your heart, not your head.

We've a perfectly good proposal to put forward, and we can put it without the need for violence.

Newland There's some hot-heads in this village. *(He looks at Aaron Harding)*

Aaron Harding Look, just because I mean to stand up for myself doesn't make me a hot-head. I can be as reasonable as the next man.

Newland So long as the next man agrees with you.

Aaron Harding See here, John Newland ...

Holdaway Let's not argue between ourselves - let's look united when we make our case.

Aaron Harding *(Sarcastically)* Our case? What's that?

Holdaway Lower tithes and higher wages.

Aaron Harding Fat chance.

Holdaway And we'll be orderly when we present it.

Heath You've not a hope. Once the villagers sniff a chance to show their strength, the vicarage will be down before nightfall, mark my words.

Holdaway We mark them John Heath, and I hope to God you'll help us prove them wrong.

Aaron Harding *(Again)* Fat chance!

There is a knock on the door, and Charles Fitt enters.

Fitt May I come in?

Holdaway *(Rising)* Come in and welcome Charles. We were just preaching caution to Aaron here.

Fitt Good - the last thing we want to see is bailiffs and militia men all over the village.

Newland D'you think it might come to that?

Fitt *(Sitting at the table)* No reason why it should, so long as there's no trouble.

Holdaway *(Looking hard at Aaron Harding)* My view precisely.

Fitt The labourers' demand for higher wages is not un-reasonable - even I as an employer can see that - but I cannot afford to pay them while the Church continues to demand the same level of tithes from me.

Aaron Harding I've never seen a starving farmer yet.

Newland Lay off, Aaron.

Aaron Harding No, listen, I'll have my say. He comes in here pleading poverty when I know for a fact that he's laid off four men this year and he's paying the rest the bare minimum.

Fitt Unfortunately I cannot control the weather, Mr Harding, and after two such abysmal harvests there's little enough for me to sell.

Heath You farmers are a mollycoddled lot - looked after by the powers that be, not like the rest of us. If the harvest is down, the prices go up and you lose nothing by it - but you still plead poverty and take it out on the labourers.

Fitt All I can say to that, Mr Heath, is that it is just as well your vision of finance is not used by those who run the country, or we would all doubtless be the slaves of the French by now.

Newland John has a point though. These things are regulated in the farmers' favour. How's it put in that *Political Register*, Robert? *(He indicates the pamphlet on the table)* "The law prohibits the import of corn until home prices have risen to 80 shillings a quarter", or some such. All to protect the farmers' pockets.

Holdaway That may be, but it's only one side of the coin. We're concerned with the drain on funds going to the Church in tithes.

Fitt And the same tithe is expected of us, year in, year out, regardless of the state of the harvest. In bad years it leaves us very little money to play with.

Heath "Little money"? You've no idea what "little money" means. You've never had to scratch in the hedgerows for your next meal and risk the gallows if you so much as trap a rabbit.

Newland And nor have you.

Heath No, thank God. But there's plenty of honest people who have.

Fitt If I may say what I came to say ...

Holdaway Go ahead, Charles.

Fitt I have agreed to see the vicar on behalf of the farmers, and argue for a reduction in tithes ...

Aaron Harding *(Again)* Fat chance!!

Fitt And we will offer to increase the wages we pay our labourers to twelve shillings a week.

Newland Aye, that's what they're demanding - two shillings a day.

Aaron Harding *(To Fitt)* I suppose you'll be getting one of those threshing machines soon, farmer Fitt, and putting even more out of winter work.

There is a general hubbub for and against this statement.

Holdaway Can we bring this meeting to order please.

The hubbub dies down.

Holdaway One thing at a time, Aaron. So you're seeing the vicar, Charles - when?

Fitt I'll go to see him first thing Monday morning.

Newland Better not make it too early - he's a man of leisure - he may not be up when you get there.

Fitt Well it will do him no harm to see that working men rise before the sun at this time of year.

Holdaway You will let me know how it goes?

Fitt I'll come as soon as the meeting is over. *(Rises)* And now I shall leave you men to discuss whatever else you feel is necessary.

Holdaway Until Monday, Charles.

Newland 'Night, Mr Fitt.

Fitt exits.

Aaron Harding *(After him)* Good riddance.

Holdaway *(Weary sarcasm)* Thank you, Aaron.

Heath *(To Holdaway and others)* You've never known a day's hardship in your life. And here you are trying to turn the protest of the poor into something that suits your own ends.

Newland You know it's nothing of the sort, John.

Heath If <u>we</u> win, <u>you'll</u> pay lower tithes - a smaller Poor Rate.

Newland If the mob gets out of control there'll be no winners.

Holdaway If we're better off than some, it's been through our own efforts not through charity.

Aaron Harding *(Angrily)* One thing's sure - with folk like you in charge, us labourers won't get any justice. Well, we'll see where we all stand when the day comes, shan't we. Good night to you. *(He exits quickly)*

Heath *(Rising)* Well, that's it then.

Newland You off to hatch plots with Aaron then?

Heath *(Moving to the door)* I might be.

Holdaway Don't make things worse.

Heath I'll not make things worse than they are. *(He exits)*

Holdaway We must keep our eye on that lot, or there'll be the devil to pay.

Newland Amen to that. *(He exits)*

Holdaway remains on stage - a pause. Suddenly there is the sound of three shots being fired. Mrs Harrison screams off-stage.

Mrs Harrison *(Off-stage)* Help! Murder!

Harrison *(Off-stage)* Who's there? Who goes there?

Mrs Harrison Come away from the window, they'll fire again.

Harrison They've run off. (*Shouting*) Cowards! Shooting women and children while they sleep.

Spotlight returns to Holdaway. Newland runs in.

Newland Someone just tried to shoot the Harrisons down at the workhouse.

Holdaway Are they hurt?

Newland Apparently not. But their clothes and furniture were torn to pieces.

Holdaway This is just the start, John. Just the start. (*They exit*)

---

7. In the Newlands' cottage, soon after

We see Mrs Newland busy sewing in front of the fire. She is a sympathetic lady with a strong character. There is a crib in the corner of the room. John Newland enters from outside.

Mrs Newland Was that shots I heard?

Newland Things aren't good. We're in for trouble I'm afraid.

Mrs Newland Aaron?

Newland Aye, Aaron for one. He bears a grudge against the vicar, the workhouse and the rest of the world it seems.

Mrs Newland One man doesn't make a riot.

Newland There's others. Half the village seems to want to do the same. Robert Holdaway's trying to organize the protest instead of just letting Aaron and his friends cause chaos.

Mrs Newland I don't know what times are coming to. Who was shot at, then?

Newland The Harrisons. They run that workhouse to line their own pockets. I think if I was them, I'd keep my bags packed from now on.

Mrs Newland Well I hope you can stop too much trouble.

Newland We'll do our best. Robert wants me to take the old horn along.

He rises and goes to take his horn down from its hook on the wall.

Mrs Newland It's seen good service, that horn.

Newland Aye, it helped topple Bonaparte, and now perhaps it can do duty nearer home. (*He gives it a trial blow*)

---

8. Inside 'The Compasses', next morning

Robert Holdaway is with his wife Sarah.

Sarah You heard about the shooting?

Holdaway stays silent.

Sarah You suspect Aaron? (*pause*) Of course you do. Or John Heath. (*pause*) Or both.

Holdaway We've nothing left to offer the likes of Harding and Heath.

Sarah So what are you going to do?

Holdaway If we can't avoid a row, then at least we can try to control it.

Sarah Why you?

Holdaway Who else would do it, Sarah?

Sarah The farmers?

Holdaway Huh! They'll watch events from the edges of the crowd and give encouragement - no more than that.

Sarah Is that all? Their presence in the crowd could have a calming influence.

Holdaway I know, but the penalty for riot is heavy, and they have much to lose.

Sarah (*Looking significantly at Holdaway*) We all have much to lose.

---

9. In Selborne Vicarage, early morning Monday 22 Nov.

It is still before dawn. We hear a cock crow. There is a loud knock at the door offstage, and we hear offstage conversation.

Fitt I wish to speak with the vicar on a matter of some urgency.

Housekeeper But Mr Fitt, 'tis not yet breakfast time - the master is still a'bed.

Fitt Then pray rouse the master and tell him - <u>ask</u> him if he would be so kind as to give me audience.

They enter.

Housekeeper So early in the morning?

Fitt It may be early for this household, but I can assure you, Madam, that the rest of the village has been up and about these last two hours.

Housekeeper Yes sir, I'll go tell the master you're here.

She goes to exit, but meets the Vicar coming in. He has obviously only just got up from his bed.

Mr Fitt, sir. *(She exits past the vicar)*

Vicar Mr Fitt, what is the purpose of this boisterous intrusion at such an ungodly hour.

Fitt Ungodly, vicar?

Vicar *(Caught off guard)* Unusual shall we say then. I do not have the habit of giving breakfast-time interviews.

Fitt Mr Cobbold, I come to you in good faith ...

Vicar I think I must be the better judge of good faith in this village, Mr Fitt.

Fitt *(Undeterred)* The purpose of my visit is simple. It is to negotiate a reduction in tithes on behalf of the local farmers. As you are aware ...

Vicar I am aware of custom and established history, Mr Fitt. It seems to me that a mechanism which has served so well and for so long to maintain the fabric of religion in this country should not be lightly set aside. Particularly so early in the morning.

Fitt We are not asking for it to be abolished, Mr Cobbold - merely that the Church should move to ease our difficulties during a particularly difficult period.

Vicar And when this so-called difficult period is ended, will you willingly concur to the re-establishment of payments back to the present level? I doubt it Mr Fitt, I truly doubt it. Reduce the tithes and we cut the very life-blood from our living Church.

Fitt Maintain the tithes and you cut the life-blood from your living congregation.

Vicar As a yeoman farmer, Mr Fitt, you command an imaginative use of words.

Fitt We don't all have to be Oxford men, Mr Cobbold, to be able to express ourselves properly.

Vicar Indeed not - I allow that others will rise from time to time to make their contribution.

Fitt I must tell you that there are those outside who would rise today. And not simply by using words.

Vicar You are referring, presumably, to rumours of recent unrest in some distant parishes?

Fitt I am sir. But not so distant - getting closer by the day.

Vicar I shall not ask how you came by such information, but would candidly observe that your manner appears to be almost threatening. Are you an outrider of the mob, come here to extract contracts from me with menaces?

Fitt My appearance at your door today is as a friend, Mr Cobbold, and with the blessing of the yeoman farmers of the parish.

Vicar Then it is unfortunate that you and your fellow farmers come at a time of such agitation. If I am seen to bend to your demands today, it would give the appearance of having surrendered to intimidation of the most distasteful kind.

Fitt I have not yet given you details of what we wish to discuss.

Vicar Nor need you, Mr Fitt, nor need you. My mind is fixed in this matter.

Fitt You would refuse to consider the very issue whose resolution could frustrate the purpose of the mob?

Vicar Then you admit that there is a mob, and that you are familiar, intimate perhaps, with its purpose?

Fitt Mr Cobbold, you are a snob - worse, you are a fool if you cannot see the hand of reason and reconciliation extended to you, even if it is only the hand of those who you regard as lower class farmers, tradesmen and artisans. I fear your obstinacy will cause many in this village to suffer much needless sorrow.

Vicar (*Speechless at first*) Mr Fitt, you will kindly leave this house at once and return to your rabble.

Fitt If that is your last word, good day Mr Cobbold. (*Exits*)

The Housekeeper looks in.

Housekeeper (*Timidly*) Would you like your breakfast now, sir?

Vicar (*Angrily*) No, Mrs Roberts, I would not like my breakfast now. (*He pushes past her and exits*)

Housekeeper (*To herself, looking disapproving after him*) Please yourself I'm sure. Someone got out of bed on the wrong side today. (*Exits following the Vicar*)

---

10. The mob gathers in Selborne, morning Monday 22 Nov.

Aaron Harding enters through the auditorium with brother Thomas and a handful of others.

Aaron Harding Today's the day lads! Today's the day we show the gentry they can't tread us into the ground. Go round every cottage in the village and make sure any man in the house comes out to join us.

His companions scatter off-stage to do this.

Aaron Harding (*To Thomas*) Not you Thomas. You and me have other things to do.

Thomas Harding We have?

Aaron Harding There'll be certain visitors here from other Parishes today.

Thomas Harding Oh aye.

Aaron Harding They want our men to go with them to Headley tomorrow.

Thomas Harding You think they will?

Aaron Harding Only if we persuade them. Our men only see Selborne - they don't see they can be part of something bigger. If every village rises up together, the gentry won't stand a chance.

Thomas Harding Don't think Holdaway and the others agree with you.

Aaron Harding They're small-minded, Thomas. No imagination.

Holdaway appears with Newland.

Holdaway Speech-making again are we, Aaron?

Aaron Harding I suppose you think you're in charge today, do you?

Holdaway Well someone has to be, to keep you and your kind in check.

Aaron Harding Listen to his lordship talking. I think we have some business at the other end of the street, don't we Thomas.

Aaron and Thomas exit.

Newland Shall I call folk out?

Holdaway Yes, blow the horn John and bring them here.

Newland gives the horn a few blasts; men start to appear from all sides, including John Cobb - they are dressed as if they had put their best clothes on for the occasion. They continue to appear throughout the next few lines.

Holdaway Gather round lads. You're all looking right smart today.

Mob 1 We'll be dealing with gentry - got to dress nice.

Mob 2 They won't take no notice of us if we're dressed scruffy like.

Cobb They won't take no notice anyway.

Holdaway You leave the talking to me. Just be there behind me at the vicarage, to back me up.

Mob 1 Aaron thinks we should visit the werk'us first.

Cobb Aye, he thinks Harrison should be taught a lesson.

Holdaway He's only doing his job, is Harrison.

Mob 2 Living off our money.

Mob 1 He's a blood-sucker.

Cobb We'll get him first, then the vicar after - what d'you say, lads?

Shouts of agreement from the mob.

Holdaway I'm not here to lead a mob of ruffians, John Cobb.

Cobb Stay away then Holdaway, 'cause we're resolved to break the werk'us and Harrison with it.

Holdaway Our quarrel is only with the vicar.

Mob 2 <u>Your</u> quarrel may be.

Mob 1 We want to get Harrison out.

Mob 2 And the werk'us down.

Cobb What d'you say, lads? Let's go to it - to the workhouse.

More shouts of agreement from the mob.

Holdaway Wait ... *(nobody hears him)* Blow the horn, John.

Newland blows the horn, but the mob take this as a signal to march.

Cobb Away!

Mob 2 Away, now!

Holdaway *(Shouting desperately)* Wait, I said!

He is ignored; Cobb and the mob march off noisily through a side exit.

Newland Do we follow?

Holdaway Not follow - catch up with the leaders, John. Stop them, for God's sake!

They both hurry off, overtaking the jostling mob.

---

11. Outside Selborne Workhouse, soon after

We hear the horn blown, and the mob enters through the auditorium.

Cobb *(Shouting)* Get the Harrisons!

Mob 1 Leeches!

Mob 2 Living on the poor.

Mob 3 Smoke them out.

Cobb Bring up the torch.

Mob 1 Who's got the torch?

Mob 2 Burn it down!

Mob 3 Smoke them out.

They all take up the chant, "Burn it down, Smoke them out", as they advance to the stage.

Mrs Harrison appears in her nightdress.

Mrs Harrison *(To her son, off-stage)* Harry! Harry, come here. Quickly.

Young Harry Harrison enters sleepily, also in a nightdress.

Harry What is it?

Mrs Harrison Coming down the road - look!

Harry *(Rubbing his eyes)* What?

Mrs Harrison Coming down the road - there's hundreds of them. Look, will you! *(Points to the auditorium)*

Harry *(Still not quite awake, peering)* Who is it?

Mrs Harrison How should I know? Does it matter? They're coming to get us.

The mob are still chanting as they approach.

Harry Burn it down?

Mrs Harrison Quick, go and pack our things.

Harry But there are people in here - old people, sick people.

Mrs Harrison Us people! Get moving will you. *(He still stands transfixed)* Oh never mind, I'll do it myself. *(She exits quickly)*

Holdaway now enters at the rear of the mob with Newland, and together they force their way down to the front as they speak.

Holdaway *(Shouting)* Stop! *(To Newland)* Blow the horn again John - get their attention.

Newland blows his horn, and the nearer chanting dies down - he blows again, and bit by bit it stops.

Holdaway Make way there. Put out those torches, we'll have no burning here.

Cobb Oh you decided to follow then.

Mob 1 The local landlord - go back to serving ale!

Mob 2 We'll be up to see you shortly - this'll be thirsty work.

Holdaway There's women and children in there - we'll have no burning.

Cobb We'll have that house down.

Holdaway We'll not hurt the innocent along with the guilty. Let me through, will you.

Cobb *(Calling)* We've come to get you, Harrison!

Mob 1 You and your missus.

Mob 2 You've robbed the poor long enough!

Mrs Harrison, on stage, makes to look out of the window.

Cobb There she is! We see you, Mrs Harrison!

Mob 1 Where's he?

There is a baying from the mob, and the chanting starts up again. Holdaway and Newland have reached the front of the mob by now.

Holdaway Hold your noise - let me talk to them! *(To Newland)* John, give them another blast.

Newland blows on the horn again, and eventually the noise subsides.

Holdaway *(Shouting)* Harrison - we want to talk with you.

Mrs Harrison *(Nervously, re-appearing)* What do you want?

Holdaway Where's your husband?

Mrs Harrison Away on business. Why?

Holdaway You'd better get out of there.

Mrs Harrison We've done no wrong.

Holdaway There's a crowd of people here think differently - I think you'd be sensible not to argue with them.

Mrs Harrison Somebody's got to look after the poor

Cobb You look after yourselves, not the poor!

Mob 1 Fat pigs!

A general hubbub starts to rise among the mob again. Holdaway raises his hand and it dies down.

Holdaway I think you'd better come down.

Mrs Harrison They'll tear us to bits.

Holdaway Not if I tell them, they won't.

Mob 1 Let's fire it now!

More hubbub begins.

Holdaway Wait! She won't come out with you all here. Give her a few hours to pack and move out.

Cobb A few hours? We want to get in there now.

Mob 1 Get out, as you are.

Mob 2 In your nightdress.

Mob 3 That'll learn her.

(During the above we see Mrs Harrison and her children climbing out of a top window, and creep away through the auditorium. Suddenly someone notices them.)

Mob 2 Look, there they go! They're getting away!

Mob 3 Quick, get her! Go on!

Cobb No, get the house!

Holdaway Wait! Move the old and sick out first.

Newland blows the horn for quiet.

Holdaway Get the old people out - who'll help me?

Begrudging offers from the mob. Holdaway, Newland and the mob remove infirm and elderly inmates.

Holdaway *(In despair)* They're tearing the roof off, breaking the furniture up.

Newland Or taking it home!

We see broken and unbroken furniture being hauled out from the stage and carried away through the auditorium by the mob.

Holdaway They'd started a fire inside, but I managed to put that out.

Charles Fitt appears from the side.

Fitt How goes it, Robert?

Holdaway At least nobody's been killed - yet.

Fitt I see the Harrisons escaped.

Holdaway Just as well I'd say. I hold them no particular

grudge. With luck this row has about run its course now.

Fitt I fear not - I hear there's a plan to march on Headley tomorrow.

Holdaway Headley? Someone's been working behind the scenes.

Fitt Will you tackle the vicar now?

Holdaway Frighten him with numbers?

Fitt Well he wouldn't listen to reason.

Holdaway Maybe the mob will make him see sense. Blow the horn, John - they've done more than enough damage here.

Newland blows the horn.

Fitt All smashed up in fifteen minutes!

Holdaway It'll be a while before they use that place again.

Newland To the vicarage?

Holdaway *(Reluctantly)* Aye.

Newland blows the horn again. They exit followed by the mob.

---

12. Outside Selborne Vicarage, soon after

The sound of the Trumpeter's horn is heard off-stage.

Robert Holdaway enters with John Newland at the head of the mob. Newland blows the horn again to call them to order, and Holdaway knocks on the Vicarage door.

Holdaway Vicar Cobbold, are you at home?

There are shouts from the mob.

Cobb Knock the door down and drag him out.

Mob 1 We should have done that at the werk'us.

Mob 2 Burn the place down.

Holdaway No mischief, I said. We can put a good case without causing a row.

There are angry mutterings from the Mob, as the door opens and vicar William Cobbold appears. He is nervous.

Vicar Mr Holdaway, may I ask the meaning of all this?

Holdaway I think you know full well, vicar. We want a reduction in tithes and an increase in your contribution to the Poor Rate.

Vicar But you know the majority of the tithe goes straight to Oxford. I have no say in the matter.

Holdaway But six hundred pounds a year goes to you. How can you justify six hundred pounds a year when others around you in the village are out of work and whole families starving?

Vicar I contribute to the Poor Rate as much as any landowner in the village does.

Holdaway No other landowner in the village is earning £600 a year. Will you take a reduction in tithes?

Vicar By how much?

Holdaway By half. We think £300 a year is quite enough for you.

Vicar Impossible.

Holdaway Oh I think you'll find it possible vicar, if you think about it for a while.

At this the Mob press forward. Holdaway raises his arm to stop them.

Vicar Do I take it you are threatening me with violence if I do not comply? I am not a mere Poor House overseer you know.

Holdaway All the labourers in the village put together would not earn even £300 in a year. I suggest you act practically, Mr Cobbold. The farmers say they will pledge to pay higher wages if you sign a document to lower the tithes.

Vicar And what about shopkeepers and tradesmen such as yourself, Holdaway. You pay no wages to labourers - yet your tithes will also be reduced. No wonder I find you here leading this petition.

Holdaway We support those we do not employ, as you well know Mr Cobbold, by our contribution to the Poor Rate. Well, what do you say?

Mutterings and movement from the Mob.

Vicar (*Looking anxiously at the Mob*) It seems I am not in a position to offer much resistance. Very well, I will sign your wretched piece of paper ...

Holdaway Good.

Vicar ... to reduce my share of the tithes by a hundred pounds a year.

Holdaway The demand is <u>three</u> hundred.

Vicar Mr Holdaway, let us be sensible about this ...

The Mob press forward again. Holdaway raises his arm again to stop them.

One hundred and fifty then. This is open robbery.

Holdaway Three hundred, Mr Cobbold.

Vicar Could you live on half your wages, Mr Holdaway?

Holdaway I could if they were as fat as yours.

Cobb Living on half my wages wouldn't make no difference to me - half of nothing's nothing, even I can figure that out.

Mob 1 Same here.

The Mob starts to crowd in and make threatening noises again.

Vicar (*Looking around*) It seems your threats leave me with little choice, Mr Holdaway.

Holdaway Threats? We've issued no threats vicar, only reasonable argument.

More threatening noises from the Mob. Cobb tries to rush at the Vicar - Holdaway pulls him back.

Vicar (*Unsettled*) You have me at a disadvantage. Three hundred it will have to be.

Cobb We'll have that in black and white.

Vicar I will have the Churchwarden write out an agreement.

Mob 1 What about giving a bit more to the poor then, vicar?

Vicar I already give my fair share to the Poor Rate.

Cobb Could you live on two shillings a day, vicar?

Mob 1 With a wife and six children to support.

Vicar As the Lord's representative, surely it is reasonable that I maintain a certain standard of living.

Holdaway Times change and standards with them, Mr Cobbold.

Vicar There I must disagree with you, Mr Holdaway. Standards must be upheld at all costs.

Holdaway At all costs, vicar?

Vicar Yes, at all costs.

Holdaway So you are not prepared to consider any increase in your contribution to the Poor Rate?

Vicar I am not, sir. You have already extorted enough from me today. I will yield no more.

Holdaway Well on your head be it. I will get the farmers here today to witness this agreement, and hope that it satisfies everyone.

Vicar And just remember, Mr Holdaway, that you will be seen as the leader of these lawless men. Whatever they do in the way of mischief will be held at your door.

Holdaway I thank you for your concern. And now we shall leave you in peace.

Cobb (*Shouting*) Tomorrow we'll do Headley.

Mob 1 With Aaron's men.

Mob 2 We'll smash the other werk'us.

Cobb Burn it to the ground.

Mob 1 Kick the Shoesmiths out.

Mob 2 Just like those Harrisons.

There is considerable support from the rest of the Mob for this idea.

Vicar I fear you are riding a tiger, Mr Holdaway. Good day to you. (*He retires into the Vicarage, closing the door*)

Holdaway So much for the concern of the shepherd for his flock.

Cobb What about that drink now Holdy?

Mob 1 Thirsty work, rioting.

Mob 2 Let's take a collection.

Mob 1 From those with money.

Cobb We'll need about £5 for a couple of drinks each.

The mob starts to ask other villagers [the audience] for money.

Holdaway (*Shouting after them*) You've already milked them for as much as they've got.

Fitt It's all right Robert, the farmers will give £2 from the Poor Rate for drinks at *The Compasses*.

Holdaway From the Poor Rate?

Fitt Aye, that should buy them a pint each.

Holdaway Is this wise Charles?

Fitt We feel it's a way to show our appreciation without becoming too involved, in the eyes of the authorities.

Newland And before the mob demand it from you anyway.

Fitt Yes well, perhaps so Mr Newland, perhaps so.

Holdaway (*Shouting to the mob*) A pint for each of you at *The Compasses* - it's on the farmers.

They exit towards The Compasses, followed by the mob.

———————

13. At *'The Anchor'*, Liphook, later that day

Mrs Harrison and family arrive, muddy and weary, just as Mrs Dowling, the landlady of The Anchor, comes out of the inn door arguing with the Captain of the 5th Dragoons.

Mrs Dowling Thirty bottles of my best gin, Captain, that's what I'm complaining about.

Dragoon Captain Madam, if you cannot keep a better watch on your liquor ...

Mrs Dowling Better watch? What am I supposed to do, stay up all night guarding it with a rifle? The store was securely locked and bolted.

Dragoon Captain Not well enough it seems.

Mrs Dowling Well enough to keep normal rogues out. Your troops used military equipment to break in.

Dragoon Captain The outcome of your lax security, madam, is that a whole contingent of His Majesty's Dragoons, sent here to help quell the unrest in these parts, has been decimated in a single night.

Mrs Dowling Drank themselves senseless on my gin and needed stomach pumps this morning to save their lives. There's military discipline for you!

Dragoon Captain You will be hearing more from the authorities.

Mrs Dowling And they'll be hearing more from me, with a bill for the liquor.

Dragoon Captain Regrettably, madam, it is your responsibility to collect money from your own customers.

Mrs Dowling (*Mimics him*) Then regrettably, Captain, The Anchor at Liphook will no longer be pleased to billet His Majesty's troops in future.

Dragoon Captain I have nothing more to add. Good day to you. (*He turns to go, bumping into Mrs Harrison*) Pardon me, madam. (*He exits*)

Mrs Dowling Arrogant, stuck up ... (*Notices the Harrisons*) What are you two doing here?

Mrs Harrison We're after a room, Mrs Dowling.

Mrs Dowling A room, eh. Selborne got too quiet for you then? Coming to see how we live life on the Turnpike? I've got a troop of drunken soldiers in there too ill to move, and a cellar floor awash with gin and broken glass.

Mrs Harrison You've had trouble then.

Mrs Dowling It doesn't take a genius to see that! What are you doing here anyway?

Mrs Harrison We've been thrown out of the Poor House.

Mrs Dowling Thrown out? Who by?

Mrs Harrison A mob came, lead by Robert Holdaway.

Harry Harrison Hundreds of them there were.

Mrs Harrison Threw the paupers out ...

Mrs Dowling Holdy? He wouldn't do a thing like that.

Mrs Harrison He was there, right at the head of them.

Mrs Dowling There's been trouble in Liphook too. Old Quarrier the magistrate, he grabbed a man from a crowd that was protesting here this morning and sent him off in chains to Portsmouth.

Mrs Harrison We'd like to stay a few nights, if you've room. Until things settle down in Selborne.

Mrs Dowling Oh I've room. No luggage?

Mrs Harrison We've lost everything except what we're standing in.

Mrs Dowling Then you'd better come in. You can help do some of the work here - starting by cleaning up the cellar.

They go into the inn.

----

14. At Selborne Tuesday 23rd November, early morning

Holdaway and Fitt enter arguing.

Holdaway Why me, Charles? There must be someone else you can find.

Fitt Nobody else we'd trust, Robert. You're well known round these parts, and well respected too.

Holdaway I'd willingly go on my own to collect other signatures of support.

Fitt But the mob won't hear of it - they want to see it happen with their own eyes.

Holdaway So it's to Empshott and Greatham, and then to Headley.

Fitt The Headley farmers are planning to meet their Rector at midday today. We want to get their signatures too.

Holdaway The mob have a different reason for wanting to go to Headley. You know that, don't you?

Fitt I had heard, yes. Another workhouse.

Holdaway Aye, another workhouse. How's it going to look when I arrive at Headley for this meeting with a mob of ruffians at my tail?

Fitt You'll do it for us though, won't you?

Holdaway It seems I have little choice, Charles.

They exit.

---

15. On the Road to Headley

The mob enter through the auditorium. John Heath, Aaron and Thomas Harding are in the lead.

Aaron Harding *(To members of the audience)* Will you contribute to the cause of the labouring man? Sir? Madam?

Heath We don't mean to threaten you with the mob here - just asking, civilized like.

Aaron Harding A few pennies won't set you back much - you can manage a few pence, can't you.

Heath Every little helps - a penny buys a starving man some bread.

Aaron Harding Tuppence feeds his family too.

Heath *(To Holdaway, who enters from the side)* Got another signature then Holdy?

Aaron Harding That's what we like to see - lots of signatures.

Thomas Harding *(To Holdaway)* Did you think this many folk would be with you, Holdy?

Holdaway I did not, Thomas. I'd intended to come alone. Have you counted heads?

Thomas Harding They've been joining us at every turn ever since we left Selborne.

Holdaway *(Looking to the stage where Henry James and others are waiting)* And more to come. Where are we now?

Heath Standford Green. That'll be old Henry James and his family, from the forest.

Holdaway You know them, John?

Heath Know of them. No-one knows them well.

Holdaway Will they be with us or against us?

Heath Oh they'll be with us.

Henry James *(Calling to them from the stage)* Who's the leader among you?

Holdaway I speak for all here.

Henry James You do? And who may you be?

Heath He's Robert Holdaway of Selborne.

Henry James *(To Heath)* I recognise you, John Heath - and some of those behind you.

Heath You know our purpose?

Henry James Oh aye, I know your purpose.

Heath You'll join with us then.

Henry James Oh I'll join you alright. There's a few more here that'll join you too.

Holdaway All yours? From the forest?

Henry James No, not all. There's some here from Bramshott, others from Conford and round about.

Holdaway We go by the ford from here?

Henry James Aye, past old Curtis's place.

Heath He's one of the local constables.

Holdaway We've no business with him - we're here to meet the farmers.

Heath You're here to meet the farmers.

The mob make it clear that they have other interests.

Holdaway To Headley then, and an end to this matter.

Holdaway and Henry James lead the cast out.

*** INTERVAL ***

16. On the Hulk 'York' - Matthew Triggs picks up the story

In the prison cell on the hulk 'York'.

Holdaway Was Headley as unhappy a place as Selborne, Matthew?

Matt Triggs Show me any happy village at the moment.

Holdaway John, you know both places - what d'you say?

Heath Rates are very high in Headley, 21 shillings in the pound.

Holdaway Is that enough to cause a riot?

Heath Doubt if you could start a riot in Headley, but once we'd got Selborne going ...

Holdaway You got it going?

Heath ... Headley followed on.

Matt Triggs That werk'us was an evil place. My uncle Tuckey was in there. It was just a business to Shoesmith.

Heath Same as Harrison in Selborne.

Matt Triggs Me and my brother William, we'd heard there was likely to be trouble there that day, so we went down first thing in the morning to get him out.

17. Outside the Headley Workhouse, 8am Tuesday 23 Nov.

We see Matthew and William Triggs enter, and move towards the Workhouse door.

Matt Triggs Come on William, you heard last night in the *Holly Bush* as well as I did.

Will Triggs So I did, but I dunno.

Matt Triggs Dunno what? Dunno that our old uncle Tuckey might get hurt?

Will Triggs They'll not let us take him out. That old Shoesmith, he's a right stickler.

Matt Triggs There'll be trouble alright if he doesn't, you see.

Will Triggs You'll be in trouble yerself if you don't get on with that job on the Rectory.

Matt Triggs The Rectory can wait - them there men from London can get on with the job without me for a while. Isn't old Tuckey more important?

Will Triggs I dunno.

By this time they are at the Workhouse door.

Matt Triggs (*Knocking and shouting*) Mr Shoesmith! (*Shouting again*) Anybody there? Mr Shoesmith!

The door opens and we see Mr Shoesmith.

Shoesmith What's all this? What d'you want?

Matt Triggs We want our uncle, old Tuckey.

Shoesmith You can't have him. I can't have inmates going in and out all the time.

Mrs Shoesmith appears at the door.

Mrs Shoesmith What's going on?

Shoesmith They've come for old Tuckey.

Mrs Shoesmith Why's that, then?

Matt Triggs We're going to look after him ourselves.

Mrs Shoesmith You never did before.

Will Triggs Ah, well it's different now.

Mrs Shoesmith Different? Why different?

Will Triggs We've heard there's going to be a row here today.

Shoesmith A row? What sort of a row?

Matt Triggs We're saying no more - let's just have old Tuckey and we'll be off.

Will Triggs They pulled the Selborne werk'us down yesterday, and it's your turn today.

Shoesmith I can't spare him. If there's to be a row he can speak up better than anyone else here.

Matt Triggs We don't want to see him hurt.

Shoesmith Then you'd best see to it that there isn't a row here today, Matthew Triggs. Look, I bear you no grudge - have a pint of my beer each, and then be on your way, eh?

---

18. In Headley High Street, later

Mr Lickfold, Headley shopkeeper, stands in a spotlight giving an eye-witness account.

Lickfold My eye, I recollect so well the day they pulled the werk'us down! The mob went round everywhere to all the houses in the morning and begged what they could. I have the shop up here by the *Holly Bush*, and they came to me and I gave them, I think it was, seven loaves and some cheese.

Spotlight moves to Mr Tend, decorators' foreman from Kennington, London, giving his testimony at the trial.

Mr Tend My name is Tend. I am a painter and paper-hanger from Kennington, London, and was at work with some of my men at the Rectory at Headley on the 23rd of November. Some men came to us that morning. Matthew Triggs and his brother were there. They told us that me and my friends must go with them to Headley Green.

Matt Triggs (*On stage*) Gentlemen, you must come with us.

Mr Tend (*Joining them on stage*) We will not. This affair has nothing to do with us.

Matt Triggs If you don't come, we'll set fire to the Rectory.

Mr Tend (*In the spotlight*) I went out to consult Mr Dickinson, the Rector. When I did the mob surrounded me and said they would murder me if I attempted to get away. I did not go after all.

Spotlight moves back to Mr Lickfold.

Lickfold I'm deuced glad I had nothing to do with it. The foreman tried to persuade Triggs to go back to his work -

Mr Tend Now Triggs come back or it'll be the worse for you in the end.

Matt Triggs Not me!

Lickfold Well, when the foreman found he couldn't persuade Triggs he writes to London for soldiers - he knew lots of languages so he wrote in Dutch -

Mr Tend They won't understand it even if they get hold of it.

19. On Headley Green, soon after

Mr Lickfold continues with his eye-witness account.

Lickfold The old gentleman, that's what we called the Rector, he was living with the Bennetts at Hilland while the Rectory was under repair. He heard what was coming, and he popped down to old Mr Ewsters, you know at Arford House. But they dragged him out and his wife too, and they brought them all up the green, and the women patted them on the back and said, "Aha! you'll come down 300, I know".

We see Rev and Mrs Dickinson shepherded onto the stage by the local Headley mob.

Matt Triggs (*Offering a paper to the Rector*) If the vicar of Selborne can manage to come down to £300 a year, Mr Dickinson, we're sure you can survive on £350.

Mr Dickinson It would appear, Mr Triggs, that this document was drawn up in advance by someone of education.

Matt Triggs Better than our village school can teach, you mean.

Mr Dickinson I mean no disrespect to Dr Holme's excellent school. But this was not written by an average hand.

Matt Triggs That's not for me to say, Rector. (*The Rector signs*) There, you've signed it, and we've witnessed it - all of us.

Mr Dickinson What do you intend to do now? This is a

dangerous mob you have assembled.

Matt Triggs These are just Headley people. Wait till you see the Selborne mob arrive. (*He sees Mr Shoesmith watching*) I said, wait till you see the Selborne mob arrive, Mr Shoesmith!

20. At Headley Workhouse, soon after

Mr Lickfold continues with his eye-witness account.

Lickfold Oh! it <u>was</u> a mob! Ah! there must have been two thousand of them, they came from all round. We saw them coming up from Standford towards the werk'us, and one of them acts as leader ...

Holdaway, Henry James and Eli Smith, a local farmer, lead the mob which enters through the auditorium.

Holdaway Halt!

The mob halts in front of the Headley Workhouse gate. Holdaway, James and Smith go up to the front door.

Holdaway (*Knocking at the door*) Mr Shoesmith!

Shoesmith (*Opening the door*) What Holdy, are you here?

Holdaway Yes, and you'd better turn out - they want to pull the place down.

Shoesmith But there are old people in the house, and children ill with fever.

Holdaway They'll be protected and taken care of. What part of the house are they in?

Shoesmith In those rooms up there, d'you see?

Holdaway Mark the windows - I'll take responsibility they're not harmed. (*To Henry James*) You'll see to that, Henry?

Shoesmith (*To Eli Smith*) I'm glad to see you're here, Eli. You're a respectable farmer in these parts - you can stop them doing this, can't you?

Eli Smith James, I've never heard any complaint of ill-treatment by you of any of the paupers in Headley Workhouse. I've done all in my power to try to dissuade the mob from doing this, but I've not succeeded, have I, Mr Holdaway.

Holdaway I mean you no harm, nor your wife, nor your goods, so get them out as soon as you can. They're all fired up - I can't hold them.

At this point, some of the mob try to rush the door. Henry James shuts the gate in front of them.

Henry James No you don't, my fine lads. No-one shall enter here at present.

Shoesmith *(To Holdaway)* You'll give us time won't you, to take out our traps.

Holdaway consults with Henry James.

Holdaway We'll give you two hours. Henry James here and his family will stay to help you move them. *(To the mob)* Right lads, away up to the Green now.

There are some disgruntled noises from the mob, but they eventually move off, lead by Holdaway and Eli Smith.

Henry James Right, Mr Shoesmith, let's get moving. Where shall we start? *(They exit into the Workhouse)*

21. On Headley Green, soon after

Matthew Triggs enters. Holdaway and the Selborne mob reappear.

Matt Triggs You've arrived then, Holdy.

Holdaway For better or for worse, aye Matthew. We started at six this morning.

Matt Triggs Doesn't take four hours to walk from Selborne - what kept you?

Holdaway We came round by Greatham, collecting signatures.

Matt Triggs Well then, let's all get back down the road to the werk'us - come on.

Holdaway Hold on, I'm here to see the farmers, not to wreck houses. Besides, we've given Shoesmith two hours to get his things out first.

Matt Triggs What? There's two hundred men here think different. They're waiting to get stuck in there.

Holdaway Two hours, we said. Henry James and his family are there helping him.

Matt Triggs That crook? Old Shoesmith'll never see his stuff again once that lot get their hands on it.

Holdaway You know him?

Matt Triggs He lives in the woods with lord knows how many in his family - scores of 'em.

Mr Dickinson the Rector enters.

Mr Dickinson Are you Mr Holdaway - come with a petition on tithes from Selborne?

Holdaway I am.

Mr Dickinson Well you'd better come with me up to the *Holly Bush* to see the farmers. We're meeting there now to discuss the matter.

Holdaway You're attending a meeting in the pub?

Mr Dickinson And why not? We are not all as narrow-minded as the vicar of Selborne. Come along.

He exits with Holdaway.

Matt Triggs So, what shall we all do for the next two hours then? Looks like Headley Fair here at the moment. Who's for a bit more pressing and collecting round the village?

There are general shouts of approval from the mob.

Mr Lickfold stands downstage in a spotlight continuing his eye-witness account.

Lickfold Then they went round begging all they could, and I sees them coming, so I says to the missis, "Fetch the gun". I puts it on the counter, and they come to the gate, and I stand at the door, oh yes, gun in my hand, and loaded, and I says, "Now what do you want?" "An ounce of baccy", says one and I says, "Here's the baccy, but you shan't have it without the money". I should have made a hole in the first one that came in, and he paid for it and they all went off quiet as lambs.

22. At Headley Workhouse, an hour later

James Shoesmith stands in a spotlight, giving his testimony at the trial, while the actions he describes are performed by the cast on the stage.

Shoesmith *(As Narrator)* The mob came back in about an hour. That was about twelve o'clock. I was upstairs with my wife in the room where the sick children were.

The mob rushed like a torrent into every room and began breaking the windows and partitions.

Shoesmith *(As himself)* For God's sake - there's children in there!

Henry James I'll put a man on the door - they won't be hurt.

Shoesmith *(As Narrator)* The rest of the mob at this moment were breaking up the doors, tearing out the windows and taking down the ceilings. The ceilings and rafters of the garret were completely torn down. In coming down I saw James Painter breaking the bannisters of the staircase.

After that they made their way through the roof and began to throw away the tiles. I saw Matthew Triggs on the roof - he is a bricklayer. The windows of the house were all torn out and the window frames destroyed. They took a copper of about 40 gallons out of the brickwork, rolled it into the yard and began to strike it with their bludgeons.

There were others in the yard breaking the gates and some were engaged in drinking my wine. There were about 30 gallons of home-made wine. I saw Aaron Harding there; he was doing nothing but drinking my wine. James Painter was astride on my cask. Thomas Harding was there and he was quite drunk.

23. Outside the *'Holly Bush'*, at the same time

Bystanders 1 & 2 enter. Holdaway comes out of the 'Holly Bush', waving a paper.

Holdaway Good news, lads. The Headley farmers have signed our agreement, and given us £7 to share between us today.

Bystander 1 Some of your Selborne mob went back to the workhouse while you were in there.

Bystander 2 They've started tearing it to bits.

Holdaway What!

Eli Smith *(To Holdaway)* And after we farmers just struck an agreement with you. You'd better go and stop them, or there'll be hell to pay.

Holdaway All you Headley People - on to the workhouse - I'll need your help.

Bystander 1 What, to stop it? No chance

Bystander 2 We'll come, but we'll join in the fun.

Holdaway Why should you want to pull down the house of these Gentlemen *(indicating the farmers in the Holly Bush)* who've just behaved so very well to you?

Bystander 1 Why not?

Bystander 2 Just try and keep us back!

Holdaway Wait! *(But to no avail, and he follows them off stage)*

24. Back at Headley Workhouse

Mr Lickfold stands downstage in a spotlight, continuing his eye-witness account.

Lickfold Oh lord, they did pull it to pieces. They pulled all the flooring up and put their sticks through the roof till the dust looked like smoke, and then they sacked the place.

Holdaway *(Enters shouting)* Come away lads, you've done enough.

Aaron Harding *(Very drunk)* Speak for yourself, <u>Mister</u> Holdaway!

Thomas Harding *(Equally drunk)* You're in Headley now. We don't take orders from Selborne here.

James Painter *(Also drunk)* Have a drink, Holdy, there's plenty left.

Eli Smith *(Entering)* What d'you think of it now, Mr Holdaway?

Holdaway It's too bad - it will hang me.

Spotlight comes up on the Judge at the trial.

Judge Your evidence please, Mr Sparrow.

We hear the testimony of Mr Sparrow, a Visitor of the Poor.

Mr Sparrow I saw the workhouse at 3 o'clock, your Honour. It was, I should say, completely demolished. It would take as much as £1,000 to repair the damage. About £200 worth of blankets and other property belonging to the workhouse were taken away, and very little of it was returned.

Judge Richard Rook, you say Robert Holdaway was the leader of this mob?

Richard Rook Oh yes sir, he was in charge. He took 'em off to the workhouse, oh yes sir.

Judge And what of Henry James?

Shoesmith Henry James assisted me to remove my goods and put them together in the yard. I believe I thanked him. I don't know where he came from. He is not a Headley man.

Spotlight on Henry James and his family, selling furniture, blankets, and other effects door to door.

Henry James Good morning, madam. Would you be interested in some nice blankets? Top quality, good as new. Recently acquired when a local hostel had to close unavoidably. Make me an offer ....

Spotlight on a final witness's testimony.

Witness At the end the Workhouse was a shell, and yet, despite the hours of violence, not one person had suffered injury.

We return to the action at Headley Workhouse. Holdaway, Matthew Triggs and James Painter enter.

Holdaway We've done enough I say. We've promises from two clergymen to reduce tithes, we've promises from the farmers to raise wages, and we've closed two workhouses. It's enough.

Matt Triggs The mob want more, Holdy. They don't want to stop now.

Enter John Heath and Thomas Harding.

Heath Bennett's taken his threshing machine away to Kingsley.

Thomas Harding He thinks it's safe there.

Holdaway We've no grudge against Bennett and his machine.

Matt Triggs <u>You</u> may not have.

Painter 'S on the way home anyway.

There is some drunken business between Triggs and Painter.

Heath I think you may not be in charge here any more, Robert.

Holdaway I've not been in charge from the beginning. I've tried to stop you all doing more mischief than necessary, but it's not succeeded.

Heath The mob <u>will</u> go on to Kingsley, Robert.

Holdaway Then I must g o with them, and see this thing to its end - one way or the other.

25. Kingsley, late afternoon of the same day

We see the Mob smashing up a threshing machine.
At the end, Holdaway enters with Heath.

RIOT! © 1993 John Owen Smith

Holdaway Have they had their fill now, John? Can we share the money out and all go home?

Heath How much is there?

Holdaway Near enough twenty three pounds.

Heath As much as that.

Holdaway How should we split it?

Heath There's people here from ten parishes. We'd best ask for a representative from each to take their fair share.

Holdaway Selborne, Headley, Bramshott, Kingsley ...

Heath ... The Worldhams, Hartley Mauditt, Empshott, Newton Valence and Greatham.

Holdaway All of those?

Heath So I'm told. And tomorrow they're off to Alton.

Holdaway Well they'll go without me then - I've done enough.

Heath I'll go and find some men I trust to take the money.

Holdaway is left alone on stage. We hear the voice of Judge Baron Vaughan at his trial.

Vaughan Robert Holdaway, we have now to look at your conduct after the destruction at Headley was effected, and we find you going with your mob to Kingsley, and there dividing among them no less than £23, the forced contributions which you had collected in the course of the day.

On that green you called out ten persons, as the representatives of the ten parishes from which the labourers had formed your assembly, in order that you might reward them for their iniquity.

And therefore, deeply as others may be stained with guilt, if a sacrifice is to be made to offended justice - and a sacrifice must be made - you are the fit person to be selected for it.

---

26. The Leaders of the Mob are arrested

The spotlight falls on Mr Lickfold again.

Lickfold Well old Mr what's his name that lived at Fowley - Mr Budd the magistrate - he got all the people together at the Anchor and swore them in you know, as special constables.

The soldiers came two days after, on horse-back two by two. I saw them coming into Headley, and I says to the missis, "How many be there?" "I don't know", says she, "forty I thought." But there was only 15 or 20. Someone said, "Here they come", and when the mob sees 'em off they ran. Some got over the hedge, and my eye, didn't the women bring the bedding back when the soldiers came!

The spotlight moves to the wife of the local magistrate, Henry Budd, writing a letter on his behalf.

Mrs Budd From Mrs Henry Budd to Mr John Bonham-Carter, High Sheriff of Hampshire, 25th November 1830
Dear Sir,
Mr Budd has opened your letter and requested me to say that Robert Holdaway is taken with Aaron Harding and John Cobb - all of Selborne - Matthew Triggs of Headley is also in custody - a very bad case - and one Harding of Kingsley. We are just returned having been out since 9 o'clock this morning. Mr Budd requests me to apologise for his not writing himself, his hands being too cold from riding all day.

We do not want any reinforcements and, as you have had more Life Guards sent to Petersfield, Mr Budd does not see any necessity for detaining the infantry here any longer.

The spotlight moves to William Cobbett.

Cobbett Will this Government shed their blood? ... The bloody old *Times* newspaper, which is the organ and perhaps in great part the property of this hellish crew, says that the labourers are starving, and that they have been cruelly oppressed; but that some of them must be made to suffer the severest penalty of the law. So **This Bloody Crew** would have men put to death for using the only means left to save themselves from starvation!

27. The Courtroom at Winchester

The spotlight moves to a Narrator.

Narrator 1   The trial of 345 men arrested throughout Hampshire began on Monday 20th December and went on for 7 days. The case of the Headley Workhouse was the first to be heard after the Christmas break.

The 'Headley 7' enter the dock together.

Usher The court will now rise.

The Judge enters and takes his place on the bench.

Usher *(To the prisoners)* You are charged with having, with divers others, riotously and unlawfully assembled at Headley on the 23rd of November and, when so assembled, feloniously pulled down and demolished the poor-house of the united parishes of Bramshott, Headley and Kingsley.

Call the Reverend Mr William Rust Cobbold.

Vicar Cobbold enters the witness box.

Att General You arethe vicar of Selborne in the county of Southampton?

Vicar I am.

Att General How long have you known the prisoner Holdaway?

Vicar I have known him for eight years.

Att General And what would you say as to his character?

Vicar I *(pause)* would rather not be asked as to his character.

Att General Thank you Mr Cobbold.

Vicar *(suddenly)* I would beg to state, however, as an act of justice to the prisoner Holdaway, that he probably saved my life and property on the 22nd by his influence over the mob that were about my house.

Att General *(Somewhat surprised)* Thank you Mr Cobbold.

The spotlight fades on Cobbold.

Att General We now call upon the defence in this case. Does any prisoner wish to make a statement on his behalf? Yes, Holdaway?

Holdaway What I did was with a good intent. I went about with the mob only to prevent them from doing any mischief. I did what I could to prevent them, but as you see I did not succeed.

Att General Your statement is noted.

Change of lighting, etc to signify the passage of time. John Newland is in the dock.

Att General We now consider the case of John Newland.

Usher I call Mr Fitt, farmer of Selborne.

Fitt takes the stand.

Fitt I wish it to be known that John Newland is, in my experience, a man of notable character, and that his actions in the recent disturbances at Selborne were an attempt on his part to mitigate the excesses of the mob.

Vaughan Do I understand from this testimony, Mr Fitt, that you were yourself present at the riot in Selborne?

Fitt I was there, your honour.

Vaughan Then sir, you ought to be ashamed of your conduct. You who, from your station, should know better, first incite these poor men to commit a very serious offence, and then you appear here to give one of them a character reference. Sir, I must tell you that you are very lucky you are not standing in the dock. I think you merit it more than these poor men.

Change of lighting, etc, again to signify the passage of time. The 'Headley 7' are back in the dock.

Narrator 1 Finally, at 10 o'clock on Thursday 30th December, the three trial judges, dressed in their scarlet robes, entered the court to pass sentence on all the accused.

Vaughan You have been convicted of having riotously and tumultuously assembled together with other persons. It is impossible to look at your conduct without seeing that you were the actual ring-leaders in that work of mischief and destruction. The law must be enforced; it travels with a slow but sure pace, and sooner or later it always overtakes the offenders with dreadful punishment.

Spotlight on the Narrator.

Narrator 1   All seven men convicted of sacking the Headley workhouse were sentenced to death.

Richard Rook *(Enters)* That Holdaway - I've done the bastard!

---

28. Reaction to the sentences

Narrator 1   There was an immediate outcry against the harshness of these sentences. The *Times* reported "most terrible distress in and about the jail, with wives, sisters, mothers and children besetting the gates every day." Petitions were sent to the Home Office from many towns in Hampshire, including one from Winchester itself signed by every trader in the town without exception.

Narrator 2 Due to this pressure, all but two of the Hampshire prisoners who had been sentenced to death, including all the Selborne and Headley men, were reprieved and their sentences commuted to transportation, mostly for life. They were taken in chains from Winchester to the Hulks at Gosport, to await transportation to Australia.

We see the 'Headley 7' being led in chains through Gosport. Among the bystanders is a father with his small son on his back.

Father Take your hat off, boy. Some gentlemen are passing by. *(Both take their hats off)*

The prisoners pass.

Father Some gentlemen, son. Don't you ever forget it.

Narrator 1   But this reprieve made no difference to the prisoners' dependants, who were left destitute to fend for themselves in their villages as best they could.

29. Epilogue

The 'Headley 7' are on stage.

Painter James Painter was never transported. After two years imprisonment in various Hulks at Gosport he was given a free pardon and returned to live with his family in Kingsley.

Henry James   Of the others, Robert Holdaway, Matthew Triggs, Henry James, Aaron Harding and John Heath sailed together on the *Eleanor* to New South Wales ...

Thomas Harding While Thomas Harding sailed on the *Proteus* to Tasmania. None ever returned.

Aaron Harding Aaron Harding married again, at the age of 55, and had two further children, Aaron and William. We know of his descendants living to this day in South Australia.

Newland enters.

Newland John Newland, 'The Trumpeter', was sentenced to 6 months hard labour, but returned to Selborne and died peacefully in his bed at the age of 77.

Vicar Cobbold enters.

Vicar The Rev William Rust Cobbold stayed on in Selborne for another 11 years, but acquired a huge mastiff for protection.

Heath Labourers' wages in Bramshott were raised, at least for a while, to ten shillings a week ...

Triggs While people in Headley were given small plots of land instead, the forerunner of present day allotments.

Holdaway   Three years later, in 1833, the dissenters at Tolpuddle in Dorset were given less severe sentences than us, the 'Headley Seven', all of them returning home after shorter periods of transportation.   Yet they caught the public's imagination and were labelled 'martyrs' by historians.

*** THE END ***

Appendix 1 - Historical Notes on Some of the Characters

The 'Headley 7': Robert Holdaway, Aaron Harding, Thomas Harding, John Heath, Henry James, James Painter and Matthew Triggs were all sentenced to transportation for their part in sacking the Headley workhouse. In fact, James Painter never sailed - but the others travelled to Australia early in 1831, never to return.

Robert Holdaway: Age 37. Carpenter, wheel-wright, hop planter, publican. Could read and write. Married.

Aaron Harding: Age 42. "Ploughs, reaps, sows". Could read and write. Recently widowed.

Thomas Harding: Age 32. Brother of Aaron. "Can plough, reap, thresh and milk". Single.

John Heath: Age 45. Farm carpenter. Could not read or write. Single.

Henry James: Age 38. Brazier, tinman, knife-grinder, soldier. Could read and write. 'From the forest', abode unknown. Widower.

James Painter: Age 36. Farm labourer. Married.

Matthew Triggs: Age 37. Bricklayer for 20 years. Could read but not write. Married.

William Rust Cobbold: Age 54. Vicar of Selborne 1813-41. From a "bilious constitution, betrayed by his yellow-tinted complexion" he was ill-qualified to bear kindly and patiently with ignorant people.

Robert Dickinson: Age 61. Rector of Headley 1818-47. A "jolly, big old Cumbrian farmer who suffered from ill-health".

John Harrison: Master of Selborne workhouse. Described as being "particularly obnoxious to the poor of the neighbourhood".

James Shoesmith: Master of Headley workhouse. A Headley farmer declared at the time that he had "never heard any complaint of ill-treatment of any paupers in Headley Workhouse".

Charles Fitt: A Selborne farmer, used here to represent all the Selborne farmers involved.

Eli Smith: A Headley farmer, used here to represent all the Headley farmers involved.

John Lickfold: Age 25. Headley shopkeeper, recently arrived in the village, but destined to become a respected figure in later years. His words here are taken largely from his comments made to a later rector of Headley, and recorded some 45 years after the event.

John Newland: Age 39. 'The Trumpeter' of Selborne. One of the surprises of my research was to discover how little he actually contributed to the proceedings, despite persistent local stories to the contrary. Nevertheless, he still became a legend in his own lifetime.

John Cobb: Age 27. Seemed to take a very active part in the proceedings at Selborne, but we do not hear of him at Headley. He, along with a number of others charged with offences at Selborne, was given a term of hard labour at Winchester, in his case 2 years.

The preface mentions 9 local men sentenced to transportation, yet the play refers only to 7 of them. The other two, Thomas Heighes and John Kingshott, were convicted of crimes which were not associated directly with our story, and therefore are not included.

For further information on these and other characters not mentioned here, read **One Monday in November** *by the same author.*

Appendix 2 - Historical Notes on the Scenes of the Play

On the Hulk 'York' at Gosport: We know the 'Headley 7' were held on this Hulk to await transportation, but it is doubtful if they would all have met and talked together as I have shown it. This dramatic licence introduces the characters and the story to the audience.

William Cobbett rides through Selborne in 1823: I resisted the temptation to make more use of Cobbett in the play. He was a major influence in events throughout the South of England generally at the time, but did not figure specifically in our local events of 1830.

A meeting of Vestry members in Selborne: There is no doubt that the Vestry and the Vicar did not see eye to eye, but the detail of this scene is pure fabrication on my part.

In Selborne Vicarage: More fabrication, I'm afraid. I know nothing of Mrs Cobbold, and suspect that the whole tone of this scene is quite improbable! But I needed some way to introduce the character of the Vicar and indicate the growing crisis outside.

At Selborne Workhouse: I have a suspicion that Aaron Harding was one of the main agitators in the village, and I try to bring in this idea here. Harrison's words are largely from his own testimony. The narrations at the end of the scene are intended to give the audience the numerical explanations of the labourers' financial dilemma in one chunk, rather than spreading it through the play.

A Back Room in '*The Compasses*': Yet more fabrication. I have ignored the fact that Holdaway was no longer Landlord of *The Compasses* (now the *Queens Hotel*), having been thrown out at the insistence of vicar Cobbold the previous year. In this scene I bring together a collection of characters to move the story along.

Outside '*The Compasses*': It is a fact that "at about 12 o'clock in the night of the same day, three guns loaded with slugs were discharged into the bedroom of Mr Harrison at the workhouse". Who knows who did it?

In the Newlands' Cottage: I wanted to introduce Mrs Newland, wife of 'The Trumpeter', and used the device of this fictional conversation between them at home. I believe it was her strong character, rather than his actions, which made him into a village legend after the events. *In a scene subsequently cut, following the Trial, I showed her walking from Selborne to Winchester during bitter winter weather, with a 6-month-old baby in arms, to see her husband in prison there.*

Domestic scene inside '*The Compasses*': There are few enough female parts in the story, so I took the opportunity to bring in Holdaway's wife here, although we actually know very little about her.

In Selborne Vicarage: Two farmers went to see the vicar during the weekend to ask his advice. We are told "he was very short with them and told them they might do as they thought fit; for his part he could do nothing". I have merely dramatised what might have happened at the meeting, using my token farmer, Charles Fitt, as the visitor.

The Mob Gathers in Selborne: I have no evidence to support the particular conversations scripted here, and in particular I suspect Holdaway was not involved in this way at such an early stage. However, I felt I had to simplify things for the audience, and decided to build on the concept of Aaron Harding versus Holdaway as being a legitimate theme. I conveniently ignored the recorded fact that the mob taunted vicar Cobbold first before moving on to sack the workhouse.

Outside Selborne Workhouse: There was great personal animosity felt against Mr Harrison, the Master of the Workhouse, but he was absent on the day of the Selborne riot, leaving his wife to face the mob. Local legend says that she fled through an upstairs window. It is my invention to give her a young son named Harry. The mob did not actually pull down the bricks and mortar of the workhouse, but they broke the fixtures and fittings, pulled tiles off the roof, and started several small fires all of which were subsequently extinguished.

Outside Selborne Vicarage: Again, facts do not support Holdaway being the leader of the mob at this stage - but he was prominent in holding back the rioters here and saving vicar Cobbold's life and property. The confrontation was well recorded at the time, and I have merely dramatised the available information. It is still not clear when and by whom the idea of going on to Headley the next day was first raised.

At 'The Anchor', Liphook: I found two casual references to *The Anchor* during my research, one stating that the Harrisons had fled there, and the other that a company of Dragoons billeted there needed stomach pumps to save their lives after they had raided the Inn's liquor store. The opportunity to add a little light relief to the play was too good to ignore!

On the Road to Headley: This scene starts at the point when Holdaway finally accepts the role of leader; he is the only man acceptable to both the farmers and the labourers. From here on, he is fighting a losing battle which is bound to end in his personal tragedy. As the interval approaches, the enlarged mob is about to enter Headley - and trouble looms.

The Interval separates the events at Selborne and Headley. In some ways the same thing happened at both places, and it was a concern of mine that we should not simply repeat the action of the first half unchanged in the second. Fortunately a number of differences were available, not the least being that the events of the Headley sacking were reported in more detail at the time, since it was this action which resulted in the transportations. Therefore a great deal more of the second half is based on verbatim accounts of witnesses at the subsequent trial than was possible in the first half.

At Headley Workhouse, 8am: We flash back in time, and see that trouble was expected in Headley that day even before the Selborne mob arrived. The early morning visit of Matthew Triggs and his brother to the workhouse comes from Shoesmith's testimony.

Headley High Street: Matthew Triggs seems to have been a trouble-maker in Headley, and the evidence of Mr Tend, working at the Rectory, was a key factor in getting him transported. Mr Lickfold ran the shop, until recently called *Headley Stores*, which commanded a good view along the length of the village High Street.

On Headley Green: I was fortunate to be shown Mr Lickfold's account of the day's events, found hidden away among the papers of a later Rector of the village, and have used his phraseology almost unchanged. His account is the only one I have seen of the Headley Rector being mobbed - for unlike Cobbold, Mr Dickinson chose not to take the matter to court.

At Headley Workhouse, 10am: Producers should be careful to show Holdaway's reluctance as a leader here. He was later convicted largely because Shoesmith's testimony was taken out of context, and no adequate defence brief was raised. When Holdaway tells Shoesmith to "turn out", it is likely he said it more as friendly advice than as an order. As an aside, Shoesmith's recorded greeting of, "What Holdy, are you here?", seems to show that the two knew each other on 'nickname' terms, and that Holdaway was probably no stranger to Headley.

On Headley Green: The meeting of the two mobs, the larger one from Selborne and the smaller local Headley one, took place, we are told, on Headley Green, about half a mile from the workhouse. Here Holdaway met the Rector as the latter "came by on his way to *The Bush*", and was invited into the meeting to be held there with the Headley farmers.

At Headley Workhouse, and Outside the 'Holly Bush': In a split scene, we see how the mob reneged on the agreement with Shoesmith, and returned early to start sacking the workhouse while Holdaway was still in the meeting at the *Holly Bush*. We have some verbatim descriptions of what went on from both Shoesmith and Lickfold, and the action on stage follows the words. When he finally arrives, poor Holdaway's desolation is complete.

Kingsley, Late Afternoon: It is a fact that Mr Bennett of Headley had moved his threshing machine to the neighbouring village of Kingsley to avoid trouble, and that the remnant of the Selborne mob now moved on there and broke it. Whether this was premeditated, or whether they just happened to find it on their way home, I don't know. But the action of the mob ended at Kingsley, and there was a handout of the money collected during the day. The labourers then dispersed. I have started to introduce the Judge from the later trial proceedings here and in the previous scene, in order to avoid the repetition of facts in the Trial scene.

The Leaders of the Mob are Arrested: There is much that could be said about the arrests, but I think it would not add significantly to the story in the eyes of the audience. Cobbett's outburst, while not made specifically about our local events, provides us with the sub-title of the play. The **Bloody Crew** he refers to is, of course, the Government not the rioters!

The Trial at Winchester: Most of the significant evidence given at the trial has already been presented in previous scenes. Here we sum up, and also show the Judge's recorded scolding of the farmers for failing to stop their labourers from rioting. The comment from Richard Rook, a Headley labourer "of infamous character" according to defence counsel, was made away from the courtroom. He was apparently a key prosecution witness, but I managed to find out very little about him, and don't know why he should have borne an apparent grudge against Holdaway.

Reaction to the Sentences: In reality the 'Headley 7' were taken to the Hulks on different days, but for the sake of simplicity, and to get them all on stage for the Epilogue, we decided to have them all walk past together.

Appendix 3 - Production Notes

The original production travelled to three different locations: two small Village Halls, and a larger school hall, each of which had its own particular limitations as to stage size and access. We used no scenery as such; only moveable properties such as a bar, chairs and barrels. Each site already had a raised stage, and we played on this in front of dark drapes, with entrances at the rear of the stage and at the front and rear of the auditorium. We also used a separate rostrum at the side of the auditorium for parts of the action, such as the appearance of the Judge, which actors could reach via the front or rear auditorium entrances.

The action was continuous apart from the one interval. We used split lighting to highlight different characters when necessary, allowing cast members temporarily out of the story to remain on the stage, or to steal away in the gloom as appropriate.

A number of the minor characters were 'doubled', for example: Cobbett and Rev Dickinson, Shoesmith and the Attorney General, the Captain of the 5th Dragoons and the Judge, Newland and William Triggs. Available bodies were also re-used where appropriate as Narrators and mob members. In the end we used 28 cast members, 16 male and 12 female.

Robert Holdaway is, of course, the key character throughout the play. Vicar Cobbold and Charles Fitt have significant parts during the first half, and Aaron Harding needs to come over strongly as (probably) the main troublemaker. Of the rest of the 'Headley 7', Henry James and Matthew Triggs have smaller but significant parts to play, and I have given to John Heath the role of co-agitator (Cobbold called both him and Aaron Harding "desperate and daring" men).

I have included Thomas Harding and James Painter mainly for the purposes of historical accuracy; they are specifically mentioned in Shoesmith's testimony of events at Headley workhouse, but I have given them only minor speaking parts.

In the second half, the story is held together largely by means of narration, and Lickfold's and other verbatim reports are supplemented by 'business' occuring on the stage. Shoesmith's description of the sacking of Headley workhouse, for example, was arranged to fit in with the choreography of the actions it described.

For our production we chose not to show the mob smashing a threshing machine at Kingsley, since we felt the destruction caused by the mob had been adequately shown to the audience during the two workhouse scenes - future directors can make their own decision on this.

I have not indicated specifically where music and other effects may be used, leaving this to the discretion of the director according to means and availability. We used local 'folk' musicians to give what we felt was the right tone to the show.

Robert Holdaway and Charles Fitt's signatures in Selborne vestry minutes of 11th April 1823